IT'S A GREAT DAY TO #BEGREAT

TEEN EDITION

JAMES EARL CRAY

It's A Great Day to #BeGreat, Teen Edition. Copyright © 2021 by James Earl Cray. All rights reserved. Printed in the United States of America. No part of this book may be reproduced, distributed, or transmitted in any form or by any means, including photocopying, recording, or other electronic or mechanical methods, without the prior written permission of the publisher, except in the case of brief quotations embodied in critical articles or reviews, and certain other noncommercial uses permitted by copyright law. Unless otherwise identified, scripture quotations are from The Holy Bible, New Living Translation, NLT.

GREAT Publishing books may be purchased for educational, business, or sales promotional use. For information, please email james@jecray.org.

Cover design: Kai Holmes-Cook

GREAT Publishing, LLC
Hazlehurst, GA

Library of Congress Cataloging-in-Publication Data
Cray, James Earl, author.
It's A Great Day to #BeGreat, Teen Edition
ISBN: 978-0-9977426-2-6

INTRODUCTION

In 1996, the number one hip-hop song was "Tha Crossroads" by Bone Thugs-n-Harmony. The movie of the year was *Independence Day*. Gas was $1.23 per gallon. President Bill Clinton had been re-elected. My favorite NFL team, the Dallas Cowboys, had just become the first NFL franchise to win three Super Bowls in a four-year span. 1996 was also the year I became a teenager. November 22, 1996, I turned 13 years old. That's when life started. Not really, but as a teenager yourself you feel my drift, right? It seems like everything changes when you hit 13.

I know some of you teens look at us adults, and assume we were never teenagers before. We can't possibly understand what is going on in your lives. Well, I hate to spoil it for you, but the truth is we were all teenagers once before. We all know the aggravation of dealing with parents, the frustration of going to school, and the fear of what's next after high school. The breakups with boyfriends and girlfriends, the pain of losing friends and the joy of making friends, the constant stress of not having anything to wear. We all have experienced being a teenager and although times have changed, technology has evolved and my experiences as a teenager from 1996-2002 are much different than what you are experiencing now at age 13 to age 19. The truth is we have all been teenagers before. And contrary to what you might think or even how boring it feels being a teenager some days, these are still some of the most critical years of your life. Your teenage years will shape the next 20 to 30 years of your life. Things you do and don't do now, things you learn and don't learn, things you experience and don't experience now as a teen, are the things that will shape your life. So, from a former teenager to a current teenager, embrace these years. Cultivate them and enjoy them. You have the rest of your life to be an adult with bills and unreal responsibilities.

That's why I wrote this devotional just for you. I want you as a teenager to embrace and appreciate where you are in life. I want you to not focus on the restrictions parents might place on you, but rather think about the freedoms you have now in these years. I wrote this devotional with all of you - between the ages of 13 to 19 - in mind. The language may vary, but the intent is all the same. If the content seems too advanced for you, go to Google. If the content seems to be too elementary for you, keep reading it anyway. Regardless of the complexity of this devotional or the simplicity of it, there is a component that makes it connect to all teenagers and that connecting piece is *divinity*. If you have watched the television show *Manifest* on Netflix, then this makes perfect sense to you. If you haven't watched it, then all divinity means for you is that God has set "it" up, whatever "it" might be in your life.

I want you as the reader, the teenager or even the pre-teen, to take the next 30 days seriously - just as you would your schoolwork, your practices, your games, your club and/or your relationship with your friends. Read one devotional each day. Focus on what you are reading. Read the devotional once in the morning and the same devotional before you go to sleep at night. If you want this devotional to help you, you have to help yourself. I'm excited for you. The next 30 days will be an amazing experience for you. ON YOUR MARK, GET SET, GO!

CONTENTS

Day 1: Discovering My Purpose	1
Day 2: Keep Standing Tall	3
Day 3: Our Day Is Coming	5
Day 4: Take Life Serious	6
Day 5: Appreciate the Previous Generation	8
Day 6: Nipsey Hussle Effect	9
Day 7: You're Closer Than You Think	11
Day 8: Control Your Emotions	12
Day 9: Think for Yourself	13
Day 10: Things Haven't Been Perfect	14
Day 11: Take Advantage	15
Day 12: You Were Born for It	16
Day 13: You're Worth More Than That	18
Day 14: Get Out of Your Own Way	19
Day 15: Let Your Gift Work for You	20
Day 16: Don't Get Distracted	22
Day 17: Are You Ready?	24
Day 18: Jesus Feels You	26
Day 19: Greater Is Ahead of You	28
Day 20: Set Big Goals	29
Day 21: Teamwork Makes the Dream Work	31
Day 22: Do Your Part	33
Day 23: Quitting Is Not an Option	35
Day 24: Follow the Leader	37
Day 25: You've Been Marked	38
Day 26: Don't Forget About God	40
Day 27: Get Up and Do Something	42
Day 28: Stop Trying to Impress People	44
Day 29: They Smile in Your Face	46
Day 30: Leave It with The Lord	48

Day 1

DISCOVERING MY PURPOSE

"Take delight in the Lord, and he will give you your heart's desires."
(Psalm 37:4 New Living Translation)

When it comes to "purpose", I'm sure you've heard this word before, right? There are so many books and authors that try to tell you about your purpose. Literally, people have made a lot of money trying to tell you something you have free access to. I believe purpose is a combination of what God created you to do and your desires. I believe God placed desires in your heart connected with what you were created to do, and that equals your purpose.

Many of us are wondering how to determine our purpose. We've read books and listened to podcasts. Many of our prayers are prayers of purpose. Even with all those things, sometimes your purpose still isn't clear. Have you ever asked God, "What is my purpose? How do I know my purpose?" Some of us have asked mentors, even parents, and as difficult as it may seem discovering your purpose is very simple. It's a matter of submission, loyalty, and commitment to God.

Psalm 37:4 tells us if we will submit or delight ourselves, and/or commit to the Lord, the Lord will give us the desires of our hearts. I believe this is the formula to discovering your purpose. Submitting to God and committing to God. This means being faithful to doing the things of God, to serving God, to honoring God. This also means going to church, attending Bible study, worshipping, praying, studying, and having communion with God. I believe this is truly the key to discovering your purpose! God says if we submit and commit to God, then God will give us the desires of our hearts. I believe your purpose rests in the desires of your heart.

Today, if you're really seeking to discover your purpose, the key is submitting and committing to God. If you're still trying to find your purpose or seek confirmation of your purpose, the key is wrapped in

Psalm 37:4, "Take delight in the Lord, and he will give you your heart's desires."

Day 2

KEEP STANDING TALL

"Listen, stay alert, stand tall in the faith, be courageous, and be strong." (1 Corinthians 16:13 The Voice)

In December 2018, I experienced one of the toughest days I've had to experience in my years as a Lead Pastor. Each year the non-profit I founded, GREAT INC., has a weekend retreat to plan and strategize for the year. It always starts on a Friday, which is a fun night. Then Saturday is our full day of planning. We typically spend six to eight hours planning our calendar for the next year. When we finish, the others usually go out and enjoy the city. This particular Saturday, like all the other retreats, I'm stuck in the hotel room preparing the sermon for the next day. This year, I was in the room preparing to start a new sermon series called "Breaking Through Poor Finances".

The next morning, I woke up at 5 a.m. and headed back to Hazlehurst to get ready for Sunday worship. I arrived at 9:27 a.m. As I walked inside our Crystal Palace Empact Center auditorium to turn the lights on and set up for worship, I noticed the auditorium was flooded. My heart dropped. It was 1 hour and 33 minutes before worship, and here I am standing and staring at 150 or more gallons of water covering our auditorium floor. Panicking, I made a call to one of my brothers and he wasn't able to come help. I called one of our greeters and my assistant to see if they could stop and grab a water pump, but it was too late. I went outside to check our piping system and when I came back inside, our praise team and my assistant had buckets and were tossing water out the side doors. I went back outside and called on God. God said, "the water won't stop, and you don't have time." I decided to move the chairs back and worship in the water. God then said, "Go change your message to 'It's Rain Check Time'!" I went back inside.

As one of our greeters walked in, she didn't hesitate. She took her shoes off and dove in the trenches asking me what to do. I gave her, and one of our executive leaders, directions and they started moving chairs. I walked to my office and heard our executive leaders lifting me in prayer.

I went into the office, put on my rain boots and sweatpants, and read Matthew 7:25. The scripture states, "and the rain fell, and the floods came, and the winds blew and slammed against that house; and yet it did not fall, for it had been found on the rock." After reading that, I walked out, inspired God's people and myself with these words, "We not only walked on water! We not only waited in the water, but we kept standing *even* in the water!"

As teenagers, all I want you to know today is that trials come. Sometimes, unexpectedly. No matter what strikes you, keep standing! The Bible says, "Listen, stay alert but most importantly stand tall in the faith!" No matter what you face this week, regardless of all your previous failures, shortcomings, and struggles, keep standing tall in the faith. Keep standing tall in what you believe. Keep standing tall in what you have established. Keep standing tall!

Day 3

OUR DAY IS COMING

"Let us not become weary in doing good, for at the proper time we will reap a harvest if we do not give up." (Galatians 6:9 New International Version)

Living for God certainly has its struggles, especially for teenagers. It can be hard. Trust me, I've been a teenager before, and believe it or not, I know the struggle. But living for God also has many perks. The issue we face is that those perks may not always be tangible. There is a chance we may not always see or feel those perks instantly. One of the greatest challenges of being a pastor is that it's hard to get people to remain committed to church and ministry. When people are living in poverty, or don't receive instant gratification or quick results from their prayers or their worship, they leave! Not out of anger, but out of weariness. People not only leave church or give up on God, but out of weariness people quit school, end relationships, stay frustrated, quit the team and are miserable all because they lose sight of the process.

The Galatians from scripture were people much like you and I, wanting to see results from their work. That's human nature. If I work, I want to see results but as with anything, Paul, the writer of this letter, gives us hope to keep pressing. He says, "don't get weary in doing good." In other words, don't get tired of working on yourself or your relationships. Don't get tired and give up on your team or your classmates or your friends. Don't get tired of reading your Bible, going to church, attending Bible study. Don't get weary of doing good. Paul says, "at the right time you will reap a harvest if you do not give up!"

My challenge to you today is this: don't stop doing good in your community, your homes, your schools, your relationships, your churches, your spiritual lives. Don't stop doing good. Keep up the good work because when the right time comes, you will reap a harvest. Your day is coming if you don't give up!

Day 4

TAKE LIFE SERIOUS

"Why, you do not even know what will happen tomorrow. What is your life? You are a mist that appears for a little while and then vanishes." (James 4:14 New International Version)

One morning, I woke up at 3 a.m. with a friend of mine on my heart. For 1 hour and 26 minutes, I sat there and drafted them an e-mail pouring out my heart, mentioning my frustrations and appreciations. As the emotional e-mail came to a close, I couldn't think of how I wanted to give my final remarks. I couldn't close it sincerely. I didn't want to just say I love you. I didn't want to say best regards. Instead, I typed "Take Life Serious, Cray!"

The line I used to close out the e-mail inspired this devotion. As teenagers you have to be more intentional about taking life seriously. Life is entirely too short, yes, even for a teenager to be mad, upset, and angry with people. Life is too short – yes, even for a teenager - not to chase your dreams. Life is too short – yes, even for a teenager – not to take risks and step out in faith. Life is too short – yes, even for a teenager – not to start over if you get the chance. Life is too short – yes, even for a teenager – not to say, "I'm sorry". Life is too short not to love again. Life is too short not to try God. Life is too short – yes, even for you – not to take it seriously!

The writer of today's scripture is believed to be James! That's a really cool name. In this portion of the book, James is intentional in mentioning to us the evil in bragging about tomorrow. He highlights that none of us really know what tomorrow will bring. In fact, we don't know if tomorrow will come. He reminds us we are no more than a vapor or a mist of air that's here today and gone tomorrow. Although many will look at this and preach about preparation for tomorrow beginning with God, the reality is that before we even look at tomorrow, we have to take today seriously! People die, accidents happen, people vanish, and we lose them, or they lose us. When you are angry, and upset or mad, fight it out and move beyond the moment with life being serious as your motivation. Doors and opportunities don't stay open forever so take life seriously enough to take a risk and walk through the door or out the door. Visions will vanish, dreams can die. Let the seriousness of life drive you to chase after dreams and accomplishments.

Today, spend time with your loved ones. Apologize to someone, forgive someone, take a chance in love, love again, step up and step out, chase a dream, go after a vision. Today, take life seriously!

Day 5
APPRECIATE THE PREVIOUS GENERATION

"Out of the stump of David's family will grow a shoot—yes, a new Branch bearing fruit from the old root." (Isaiah 11:1 New Living Translation)

When I first read this scripture, it jumped off the pages at me. Primarily, because it's the first verse, and secondly because of this part of the scripture, "A new branch bearing fruit from the old root." Although I'm aware the focus of this scripture is to highlight the fact that a new King is coming who will be righteous and will be from the family bloodline of Jesus, I'm also intrigued by the revelation God gave me concerning the second part of this scripture. Appreciate the previous generation. You know, the old people.

There is such a gap between generations that it has nearly made it impossible for the "old people" (the older generation) and "young folks" (the younger generations) to coexist. The older generation is too impatient to deal with the new generations' behaviors and immaturity, and the younger generations are too stubborn to listen to the older generation. This has widened the gap and more dangerously it has affected the appreciation the older generation deserves.

The second part of chapter 11 verse 1 is a reminder that "you" as a teenager (new generation) are only able to bear the fruit that you bear because of the roots of the older generation. Blacks, Whites, Hispanics, et al., can only share the same classroom because of the fruit from the previous generation. The only reason you can vote at age 18 is because of the fruit of the previous generation. Your new generations should be more appreciative of the roots and fruit of the previous generations. The freedoms you have, the access you have, all these are fruit you bear from old roots.

Today, I want you to be reminded that you are in the positions you are in because of the old roots. All of us should find someone older today and tell them how much we appreciate them for being the root that allows us to bear fruit. Appreciate the previous generation!

Day 6

NIPSEY HUSSLE EFFECT

"Herod had arrested John. He had tied him up and put him in prison because of Herodias. She was the wife of Herod's brother Philip. John had been saying to Herod, "It is against the Law for you to have her." Herod wanted to kill John. But he was afraid of the people, because they thought John was a prophet. Herod had John's head cut off in the prison." (Matthew 14:3-5, 10 New International Reader's Version)

Sunday, March 31, 2019, news flashed across my iPhone screen that rapper and community activist Nipsey Hussle had been shot in front of his Marathon Clothing store in Los Angeles, California. Moments later, Twitter revealed he had officially been pronounced dead. Although, I had never heard of Nipsey Hussle prior to this event, the continuous content of the rapper and activist flooded all my social media timelines. I instantly became intrigued and started doing my research only to find out Nipsey Hussle was the post-modern version of Malcolm X, Huey P. Newton, and Tupac Shakur all in one. If you're too young to know them, then Google them. Nipsey, like all those men I mentioned, was a radical community organizer. He was on the verge of unlocking some truths to those in power through a documentary on Alfredo Bowman, also known as Dr. Sebi. Dr. Sebi is a Honduran herbalist and self-proclaimed healer who died upon his release of the self-proclaimed cure to HIV, cancer, and several other severe illnesses. There has been great conspiracy behind the sudden sickness and death of Dr. Sebi as there is now great conspiracy behind the death of Nipsey which also ties Nipsey to the conspiracy driven deaths of Malcolm X, Huey P. Newton, and Tupac. When you're a threat to power, there will be a threat to your life!

The focus scripture for today introduces John the Baptist, the forerunner for Jesus, who has discovered a secret within the government. The King, who was Herod Antipas, was conspiring against his brother Philip to marry his wife Herodias. The information, the secret, had been revealed to John, and unlike other leaders who had remained silent about the information, John confronted both powers that be, Herod Antipas and

Herodias. John began shining light on their wrong. In an attempt to silence John from exposing Herod's government, Herod had John arrested; he was afraid to kill John but used prison to silence him. In this same chapter, at a birthday party, the opportunity came and Herodias who served as an agent of Herod's government pushed Herod to silence John once and for all. Verse 10 mentions John's head was cut off; he was killed.

Today, as a teenager, don't miss the moment of what has hurt America for centuries – the killing of the voices! In my opinion, prison hasn't been used enough for corrections. It's been used more as a silencer and when the silencer isn't working, death is the only option. Like Jesus, John, Malcolm, Huey P., and Pac, Nipsey had a message of truth to power and anytime the threat gets too close, the threat has to go! Leadership isn't about fame and prestige, but true leadership is grounded by this question: will you put your life on the line to expose the truth about power?

Day 7

YOU'RE CLOSER THAN YOU THINK

"Finally, they entered the region of Zuph, and Saul said to his servant, "Let's go home. By now my father will be more worried about us than about the donkeys!" But the servant said, "I've just thought of something! There is a man of God who lives here in this town. He is held in high honor by all the people because everything he says comes true. Let's go find him. Perhaps he can tell us which way to go."
(1 Samuel 9:5-6 New Living Translation)

Statistics have proven that most car accidents happen less than a mile away from home. Meaning most people get in accidents when they are close to their destination. Statistics also prove that a high percentage of high school students drop out of school in their last year, and a high percentage of college students drop out with only three or less semesters to go! Simply suggesting that many of us stop, end, or shut down stuff when we are close to our destination.

1 Samuel speaks to this exact reality. Saul has been sent on a mission to find his father's donkeys. He travels with his servant all day through four different areas or towns. When Saul and his servant reach Zuph, the final city, Saul seemingly becomes frustrated and is ready to go back home, not realizing he was just a few miles from meeting his destiny.

I want to encourage you today! Don't stop now. You're closer than you think. It may not seem like it or feel like it. It might be getting tougher. Trust God in the process and push through the pain and frustration, you're almost there! Look ahead, you're closer than you think!

Day 8

CONTROL YOUR EMOTIONS

"Better to be patient than powerful; better to have self-control than to conquer a city." (Proverbs 16:32 New Living Translation)

In a moment of honesty and transparency, the last few years have been emotional battles for me. Why haven't I done anything, you ask? Because I didn't fully understand what was happening, but now I get it. Emotions are extremely tricky, and we sometimes aren't even aware we are emotionally out of control until it's too late. Controlling our emotions is much more than not getting angry. Anger is just one of 27 distinct emotions. One of the trickiest emotional failures is when we allow ourselves to give emotions to things that don't deserve our emotions. In deeper thought, maybe you have invested emotions into things and/or people who aren't aware of your emotions. That's unhealthy. That's emotionally out of control.

The focus scripture states, "Better to be patient than powerful; better to have self-control than to conquer a city." This is relevant in more ways than one, but the primary area of relevance today is that impatience and a lack of self-control often are the root issues to the loss of control in emotions.

Today, through prayer time, meditation, healthy conversation, exercise, laughter, and through quiet time, redirect your attention, regain your focus, place your trust and your heart in the hands of God. Let God build your patience and ask God for self-control! Life is too short and too valuable to lose control of your emotions. And before you start asking – yes, even you the teenager – needs self-control.

Day 9

THINK FOR YOURSELF

"For as he thinketh in his heart, so is he." (Proverbs 23:7 King James Version)

In my life, I've learned a valuable lesson about perception. For most of my life, I was taught to not listen to preachers like Creflo Dollar, Kenneth Copeland, Jesse Duplantis, and Jerry Savelle. Most of these guys you may not know. Again, Google is your best friend. I was taught these preachers were prosperity preachers, all they wanted was money, and they were false teachers. I mean the things I heard about their style of preaching was ridiculous, but because the voices around me were so influential, and I respected those voices, I didn't think to look into things for myself. I just went with the thoughts of other people and let their perception become my perception. There was one week as I was preparing for Superseed Sunday at Empact Church. I decided to listen to messages from each one of them about seedtime and harvest. To my surprise, there wasn't any false use of scripture. They weren't asking for my money. They weren't being manipulative. They were simply teaching the law of sowing and reaping.

This brought me to the place where I am today. The writer of this scripture says, according to the King James Version of the Bible, "For as he thinketh in his heart, so is he". In other words, we are what we think. The French philosopher, René Descartes, said "I think, therefore I am" and the fact is, today, we must start thinking for ourselves!

Don't allow the perception of others to cloud your thoughts. Think for yourself! Don't let your circumstances like school, or the people talking about you at break, any of those teenage things cause you to get off track. Think for yourself! Don't allow negative influences to control your thoughts. Think for yourself!

Day 10

THINGS HAVEN'T BEEN PERFECT

"But what is perfect will someday appear, and what isn't perfect will then disappear." (1 Corinthians 13:10 Contemporary English Version Interconfessional Edition)

I have long wrestled with God on the idea: If you (God) are so perfect, and after everything you created, you looked back and said it was good. Then God, why does this world have so much imperfection? Why does my individual life have so much imperfection? If a perfect God sits high and looks low, how can so much stuff be imperfect? If God could send a pure and perfect vessel like Jesus, if God can speak to an empty universe and call light into it with one statement, then, God, why are there so many imperfections in the world?" I have often asked God this question and I have often received the same response, "It won't always be this way!" And that helps me to remember things haven't been perfect, but they won't always be that way! Have you in your young life ever asked God similar questions?

When I look at 1 Corinthians 13:10, it always confirms for me what God shares with me whenever I have my moments of questioning imperfection. I'm fully aware that Paul is the writer of this scripture. I'm also aware he has a set target audience. I'm also aware of all the other theological jargon surrounding this scripture, but when I read this scripture, it gives me security that when Jesus arrives, his perfection will cast out all imperfections!

Today, teenager – yes, you who's reading this - as you seek to understand and get a grasp on the things that are imperfect in your young world or the things that may be imperfect in your life, be reminded to invite Jesus into your life. Simply ask him to come because when the perfect one – Jesus - comes all things that are imperfect must disappear!

Day 11

TAKE ADVANTAGE

"Make the most of every opportunity in these evil days." (Ephesians 5:16 New Living Translation)

I'm sitting outside the gates of "The Perch" at Kennesaw State University awaiting my "Boyz" (my mentees) to arrive at the Mega Camp. The Mega Camp is the football camp where they have an opportunity to showcase their talents for college scouts. I'm watching hundreds of young men, both Black and White, walk through the gates. Some of them have a fire in their eyes, and others look like they are only here because their parents or coaches made them come. I see some young men that pass the eye test meaning they look like good football players, then I see some guys that look like they probably should be applying online for the school's merit scholarships. There are also some guys that look in between. They look like they could be good, or they could be terrible. The fact that all these young men are here despite how they look, despite what walk of life they come from, the one thing they all have in common is an *opportunity*! Although there are nearly 50 college scouts here, they only need to impress one! Today, they have the *opportunity* to impress a college team, but they have to make the very best of this opportunity. They must take advantage!

This speaks to your young life! Some of us don't look like what we've been through, but many of us don't look like what God has in store for us either. You may be tall, or you may not be tall enough. You may be very smart, and school comes easy for you, or you may struggle some. Regardless of what your status might be, one thing you have in common with all other teenagers is an opportunity. With that being said, like these young men walking through these gates, we all have been given an opportunity at something today. Whatever opportunity you have, make the best of it! Take advantage! You don't have to impress everyone, just impress one!

Day 12
YOU WERE BORN FOR IT

"I knew you before I formed you in your mother's womb. Before you were born, I set you apart and appointed you as my prophet to the nations." (Jeremiah 1:5 New Living Translation)

As I watched the 2019 NBA Draft, I was moved by several things. The first thing that moved me was the fact that the first five to 10 picks of the draft all had a strong father presence in their lives that they honored. This was a joy and a blessing to see because these young men were all Black men, and the consensus on Black men is that we all grow up without fathers. To see the strong presence of fathers in the lives of these young men, it blessed and moved me. I was also moved by the pure athletic ability and the gift of these young men. It was absolutely amazing to watch the highlights of some of these young men as they were being drafted. It was raw and pure talent. The eye-opening factor to this natural, raw, and pure talent, was that the majority of these young men were still teenagers. To see 19-year-old young men this gifted talk about the commitment they made since age four and nine blew my mind, but it also said to me that these young men were born for this game.

This brings me to this spiritual thought. God has given all of us a specific gift or talent. We are gifted to do something like no one else can do, not because we are better than they are, not because we have more favor, but simply because we were born for it. When we meet Jeremiah in the focus scripture, Jeremiah is the pastor of a small town called Anathoth. Pastoring is his position, but according to the vision Jeremiah has, he was born to be a prophet. God told Jeremiah, "Before I formed you in your mother's womb, I knew you. Before you were born, I set you apart to be a prophet." He was born for it.

Today, even as a teenager, it's time to discover what God has placed in you. The gift, the talent, whatever it is God has called you to do, walk into it because what God called you to do, you were born for it! Before you were formed, God knew you! Before you were born, God set you apart for the specific thing you are called to do. You were born for it! Take note of this and write it someplace. Your *passion* is what you like to do. Your *gift* is what you can do. Your *calling* is what you are supposed to do.

Day 13

YOU'RE WORTH MORE THAN THAT

"For you created my inmost being; you knit me together in my mother's womb. I praise you because I am fearfully and wonderfully made; your works are wonderful, I know that full well." (Psalm 139:13-14 New International Version)

Worth and self-value are two of those things we hear or talk about often, but we never seem to go deeper. We visit them on the surface. We have conversations, seminars, conferences, small groups, empowerment sessions, classes, and so many other things that speak about our need for understanding our self-worth and value. All these things are great until you get to school, and people make you feel worthless, or go to events that shatter your self-value, or when situations occur that will kill your self-esteem!

The reality is that there are many teenagers around you who suffer from self-esteem issues. You may even be one who suffers with self-esteem issues. I believe some of the feelings of worthlessness or low self-esteem come from young people like yourself placing too much value in the opinions of other people and not in the opinion of God. I know that sounds cliché but it's a fact. If we think about the scripture today, this psalm writer has given you the basic formula to building confidence in your worth and self-value. The formula is simple: you have to remind yourself that God took specific measures to create you.

The psalm writer wants us to remember God created us inside and out, while we were in our mother's womb. God fearfully and wonderfully made us. God's work in making us was wonderful and well. So as tough as it may be, remember you're not bound to the opinions of other people. Your value is not graded by your mistakes, and your worth is not measured by your friends and classmates. The truth is you're worth more than an opinion. You're worth more than a failed test. You're worth more than a shortcoming. You're *worth* more than that!

Day 14

GET OUT OF YOUR OWN WAY

"The truth will set you free." (John 8:32 New Living Translation)

As I was thinking of what to share with you today, several themes came to mind. "Stop Trying to Do It by Yourself" is the one I heard the loudest. Then this thought popped up: How often in life do we stand in the way of our own progress? Of course, when I heard this, I instantly started thinking about certain behaviors and characteristics that hinder young people. For example, bad attitudes, poor effort, laziness, poor attention to details, fear, etc., but those things don't equate to today's blockage of progress. Dishonesty was the term that blew through my mental ceiling. Although those other things play major roles in your progression or the lack thereof, I noticed they can be rooted in dishonesty.

So often, our stagnation or inability to prosper comes from the fact we lie and aren't truthful with ourselves. If you need help moving a table and someone asks you if you need help, but you say I got it. Well, guess what? You weren't honest, and now the table won't get moved. How many of us have left metaphorical tables in the same place because when help was offered to move them, we said "we got it"?

Thinking about this made me look at John 8:32 from an entirely different perspective. I've always thought freedom comes when I tell someone else the truth, or when I know the truth about something. Today, I've come to the realization real freedom is when you are willing to look at yourself in the mirror and be real and honest with yourself. We must be real about our pains, our past, our feelings and emotions, where we are in life, who we are becoming vs. who we want to be. We have to be honest about the tables in our lives. Do you need help moving any tables? If so, get out of your own way! Dishonesty with self will hinder your next move!

Day 15

LET YOUR GIFT WORK FOR YOU

"Giving a gift can open doors; it gives access to important people!"
(Proverbs 18:16 New Living Translation)

Our scripture today is more traditionally quoted as, "A man's gift makes room for him and brings him before great men." I've referenced this scripture from the perspective of gift as "talents". Our talents or gifted abilities will make room for us and bring us before great men and women. It can still spin that way, however, after studying and reading closer a new revelation and perspective were revealed to me.

Our "Gift" - a thing given willingly to someone without payment; a present - will make room for us and bring us before great men and women. So, it's partially true when we say our talent will make room for us, because we can't just possess the talent. We have to give it or use it. Using it then opens the door and gives access.

Then there is the new revelation. Your "gift," your "present," your "generous offering" to someone will open doors and give you access to important people. I'm reminded of a Bible story about a man named Saul. His father's name was Kish. One day, Saul and his servant were out looking for his father's donkeys that were lost. They heard an important man, or a holy man might be able to help them find the donkeys, so they thought about going to him. Saul said to the servant; "If we go, what do we have to give him?" This story always registers with me, because Saul understood the giving of his gift would open the door and give him access to this holy and important person. This is also why the Magi brought gifts to Jesus. They knew gifts gave them access.

My point for you is this: start letting your gifts work for you. Both your talents when used and your presents when given, will open doors and give you access to important people. These principles aren't just made-up thoughts and words, this is scripture. Our abilities when used and our presents when given, will give us access. Start letting your gifts work for you!

Day 16
DON'T GET DISTRACTED

"But Lot's wife looked back as she was following behind him, and she turned into a pillar of salt." (Genesis 19:26 New Living Translation)

Growing up in the church as a teenager, it was embedded or programmed into many of us, myself included, that if anything went wrong, if a bad accident happened, if a bad storm hit, if failure occurred, if divorce took place with parents, any and everything that was bad or negative, we were taught it was the devil. That old devil, that nasty devil, that evil devil. I think I heard that more growing up than I heard of how great Jesus is. Interesting, right? But it's a reality. If you listen close, you'll hear people give the devil credit for everything that went left in their lives. Many of people's distractions were and are blamed on the devil.

As I got older, I began to realize that – although, the devil is the thief that comes to kill, steal, and destroy – the devil isn't responsible for all the distractions happening in our lives. Some of the distractions that take place aren't the devil, but they're distractions we cause on ourselves by the decisions we make. Why is this important to you, as a teenager? Well, I believe if you understand now, at your age, some of the problems that might be happening in your life aren't just the devil; some of them are from your own mistakes. As you grow older, my hope is that you will make better decisions resulting in better outcomes in your life.

In Genesis 19, Lot was given specific instructions by angels to leave the city of Sodom. The angels insisted Lot leave the city along with his family. God had sent them to destroy the city, because the wickedness of the city had reached God. In other words, God was tired of the people being evil, so God was planning to destroy the entire city. Lot called his daughters and his wife together while still unsure about leaving the city. They were snatched up by the angels and taken outside the city. When the angels got them safely outside the city, they told Lot, his wife, and his two daughters to run for their lives and to not stop or look back. They were told by God's messengers to go, and to not get distracted. As they ran, Lot's wife stopped and looked back, and she turned into a pillar of salt. When she got distracted by whatever appeased her from their past, and decided to disobey God's instruction, God prevented her from moving forward.

What I'm saying to you today is don't miss an opportunity to move forward because you've allowed yourself to get distracted. Listen to the directions of God through God's messengers: your parents, your teachers, and your mentors. Get locked in, focus, and don't get distracted!

Day 17

ARE YOU READY?

"Be ready in season and out of season." (2 Timothy 4:2 New American Standard Bible)

As I was sitting in my bed one morning, about 6:17 a.m. desperately searching my brain for devotional material, the only thing that surfaced and resonated with teenagers and the things happening in our world, was the thought "It's Time to Get Ready". As much as I wanted to make that thought about gaining and prospering and getting more blessings, it kept popping up as a warning instead. I really wanted my thought to open the door for me to tell all teenagers it's time to get ready for your scholarship, your new boo or bae, your new fit, and your new money, but that wasn't the thought. As much as I want to tell teens to get ready for those things, I kept hearing it's time to get ready for things to be difficult, it's time to get ready for the storm, it's time to get ready for the fight, it's time to get ready for the unpredictable. The question is: are you ready?

When I glanced at the scripture that morning, all I saw were the words "Be Ready". I was fully aware that the full context of the scripture speaks to preachers. Nevertheless, that morning this small portion of this scripture spoke volumes to all teens. Be ready in season and out. At all times, be ready!

It was early fall, and Melissa had prepared her clothes for the next day of school. Her little brother who always came in her room and aggravated her before school, came in the room behind her. Although the weather was predicted to be in the high 60s, he laid out a jacket, scarf, gloves, rain boots and an umbrella next to the clothes Melissa laid out. When they got dressed for school the next morning, at no surprise the weather was in the high 60s just as Melissa had suspected. In frustration she asked her brother, "why did you pull out all this stuff? The jacket, scarf, gloves, rain boots and an umbrella, with a smile the opposite of her frown." He told her, "I know how difficult it can be trying to get ready in the morning. So just in case the weather changed, I wanted to be prepared."

The moral of this story is, as the scripture says, "Be ready in season and out of season!" Even on the most beautiful fall days of life, keep an extra jacket, scarf, gloves, rain boots, and an umbrella with you at all times. *Be prepared!* Save some money for a rainy day. You never know when you'll need it. If you're not the starter on the team yet, always know what's going on in the game just in case you get called into the game. Read, pray, focus on being a better version of yourself. You never know who you'll meet. If you stay ready, you don't have to get ready! Question is: are you ready for an attack of the enemy? Are you ready if you get put in the game? Are you ready if Jesus came back today? Are you ready?

Day 18

JESUS FEELS YOU

"For we do not have a High Priest who is unable to sympathize and understand our weaknesses and temptations." (Hebrews 4:15 Amplified Bible)

Some days are very emotional days, particularly after I preach! In 2020, I preached under the third most emotional day in my 14 years of preaching! The most emotional was earlier in 2019 when I preached at the first funeral of one of our church partners who I loved dearly. The second was January 2015 after finding an emotional letter from my father that was written on the same day nine years prior! Then came this moment. The heavy emotion of Ahmaud Arbery, Breonna Taylor and George Floyd. At the time, I had been alive for 36 years. (No, I'm not a teenager anymore, but I have been a teenager, so I know how it works.) The previous eight years before these murders took place, I had seen some horrible acts of hate crimes and police brutalities, but these three hit me differently. They were closer to home and closer to heart.

I woke up tempted to shut our church down because I didn't know if I had the strength or the words to say and inspire people that day! But then Hebrews 4:15 came to me, "For we do not have a High Priest (that's Jesus) who is unable to sympathize and understand our weaknesses and temptations." All this verse screamed out to me is that Jesus feels you! When God gave me that assurance— that no matter what I feel, Jesus can feel it - that was my push to go!

Today, I want to encourage you that there is NOTHING, even at your age, that you're feeling that Jesus can't feel! All your pains, your worries, your concerns, all your struggles, all your weaknesses - Jesus understands them, and he can feel them! When you feel like giving up, Jesus feels you! When you feel like quitting, Jesus feels you! When you are heartbroken, Jesus feels you! When you are distracted, Jesus feels you! Every temptation and every weakness, Jesus feels you! Keep going, and let your motivation be that you are not the only one who can feel what you feel. Jesus can feel it too!

Day 19

GREATER IS AHEAD OF YOU

"Lot was dragging his feet. The men grabbed Lot's arm, and the arms of his wife and daughters—GOD was so merciful to them!—and dragged them to safety outside the city. When they had them outside, Lot was told, "Now run for your life! Don't look back! Don't stop anywhere on the plain—run for the hills or you'll be swept away." (Genesis 19:16-17 The Message)

In this biblical account of Lot (we have mentioned him before), he is living in the city of Sodom. We have mentioned that place before too. Two male angels come to his home to visit. While they are there, all the men of Sodom come to Lot's home with the intention to rape him. When the male angels saved Lot and he escaped the wrath of these mad men from Sodom, the angels told Lot he and his family needed to leave there because God was about to destroy Sodom and Gomorrah. Lot's daughters were all engaged but their fiancés took God's word as a joke. Lot was instructed by the angels to leave, get his wife along with his two daughters, and go. Like many of us in the places and situations we are in, Lot had so many ties to Sodom that made him hesitant about leaving. According to The Message translation, God literally drags Lot and his family safely away from the city and tells them, "Run for your life and don't look back".

As teenagers, it is easy to find yourself thinking and acting just like Lot. We can literally be on a sinking ship or at a dying church, on a dysfunctional team, in a toxic relationship, in a negative environment and we will hesitate to move. Today, my prayer is that God will literally drag you out of some comfortable dying places and push you into the direction of your purpose and calling. The message God was sending Lot and his family, and that God is sending you, is to focus forward and not look back. Greater is ahead of you than what is behind you. Greater opportunities, greater people, greater places, greater grades, greater breakthroughs. Greater is ahead of you so *focus forward* even if you must drag yourself forward.

Day 20

SET BIG GOALS

"Though your beginning was small, your latter days will be very great." (Job 8:7 New Revised Standard Version)

It's 3:47 a.m. one morning. I'm wide awake. I usually wait until 5:00 a.m. to get my day started and 6:00 a.m. before I call, talk, or text anyone, depending on who it is. Some people have special access to me. But on that morning, I couldn't sit there until 5 or 6:00 a.m. I began texting one of my best friends about dreams and future goals. In our conversation, it struck me that it's easy to talk about accomplishing and achieving things, but I had to really ask myself, "does my passion and desire match what I want?"

After the conversation with my friend, I pulled out my Bible. Well, I opened my Bible app. I found Job 8:7, Lexham English Bible translation, "Though your beginning was small, your end will be very great." It reminds me of another verse, Zechariah 4:10 "Do not despise the day of small beginnings". Both verses provide something I've never paid attention to. As encouraging as both scriptures are, they provide a promise that our ending has the potential to *be great*! (That's definitely a play on words. #BEGREAT is my thing.) When I read the verse, I got excited but then I thought as much as it is a promise and there is potential for the future to be bright and filled with greatness, you have a responsibility on your end.

Since God has promised you greatness in the future, then the requirement for you is simple. You must have a plan for your future, that's first. Secondly, you must have an idea of what you are going to strive for in the future. So, the big question today is, what do you have in mind to go after in your future? Once you figure that out, you will match God's promise that your future can potentially be great.

God has provided and confirmed the promise that your future has the potential to be great, but you can't just sit there expecting God to make something *great* that's not there. Today, take the time to think of the biggest dream, goal, or aspiration you could accomplish. Write it down, and trust God that when the verse says your end will be greater, it will actually be greater.

DAY 21

TEAMWORK MAKES THE DREAM WORK

"He was greatly surprised, because the people did not have faith. Then Jesus went to the villages around there, teaching the people. He called the twelve disciples together and sent them out two by two. He gave them authority over the evil spirits." (Mark 6:6-7 Good News Translation)

As a pastor with a big dream to have a large church with a lot of people attending, the verse today hits different. God gave me a vision in 2016 to start five churches in five cities. I was excited about this vision, but the challenge that came with it is how would I be able to pastor all five churches. Not knowing through my style of leadership that God was giving me a model of how to do the very thing that had become a vision, or for a better word, it had become my dream. God had me establish an executive leadership team. Through trial and error, we built a team that handles all the day-to-day tasks. As God moves me around the world, the team is equipped and experienced enough to step up and handle all the responsibilities!

When you look at this verse today, I want you to think of your short journey in life. When I read it, it made me think of my current journey. I look at how God has given me this executive team model of leadership to help me accomplish my dream. Looking back at my journey, it is clear that years ago God was preparing people to join me in leadership to carry on the vision and reach this dream. In this verse, Jesus has created the same model. Well, if we are honest, Jesus is the originator of the model. I kind of borrowed it from him. Nevertheless, this verse shows Jesus' team - the disciples. When Jesus was preparing to move around or transition, he gave his team the authority to handle the day-to-day task. Mark 6:7 says, "Jesus called the twelve disciples together and sent them out two by two. He gave them authority over the evil spirits." Jesus had trained them. They were equipped and experienced enough to carry on the vision and the ministry.

Today, as you think about your dream, and what it takes to accomplish your dream, always be mindful that every dream requires a plan and sometimes it requires a team. The disciples were Jesus' team. My team is the executive leadership team. Do you have a team? Who are you hanging out with? Can those people add to your dream?

DAY 22

DO YOUR PART

"If a brother or sister is without clothes and lacks daily food and one of you says to them, "Go in peace, keep warm, and eat well," but you don't give them what the body needs, what good is it? In the same way faith, if it doesn't have works, is dead by itself." (James 2:15-17 Holman Christian Standard Bible)

On September 26, 2020, we had a service at Empact Church of Hazlehurst called "The Flip Script – Sledgehammer Faith service"! We were in a series called "You Gotta Have Faith" and we were talking about "Sledgehammer Faith" that week. We called it "Flip Script" because as you know most church services are Sunday morning at 10 or 11:00 a.m. We flipped it and started service at 7:00 p.m. That's where the name comes from. The following day, I could not stop thinking about that service. I was so stuck on the idea that faith, if it doesn't have works, is dead. I had to share it.

What does this mean for you as a teenager?
1. Faith - what you believe in or what you believe is going to happen before you can see it happening. That's faith.
2. Works - these are the things you must do to make sure what you are believing in or believing for will happen.

For example, if you're believing to one day become a college or professional athlete, that's faith. The works part is you playing well, getting the right grades, and working hard. If you plan to be an actor, film director, nurse, doctor, engineer, whatever you're dreaming for, that's faith. The things you have to do to reach these dreams, that's the works part.

In James chapter 2, it tells a short story about a faith scenario. The scenario is designed to really challenge where we are in our faith. Now, let me give you a scenario: suppose you know a girl named Breonna, and she goes to your church or your school. One day, she tells you she doesn't have any good clothes or that she needs some clothes. Suppose you see a man named Lance sitting outside of Walmart in need of food to eat. Your response to them is, "I'm praying for you, go in peace, and be warm." As the writer in James 2 asks, I'm asking you, "What good is that?" It's faith without doing anything. That's just like having faith without works, which is dead. In other words, your words and prayers are pointless if you don't offer help.

My question to you today is, "what are you doing to help someone else?" The world, your school, the community, needs more than faith. They need more than prayer. The world, your school, and the community need you to help. You have a responsibility, and that is to help those who may need your help. Are you doing your part?

DAY 23

QUITTING IS NOT AN OPTION

"You pushed me into this, GOD, and I let you do it. You were too much for me. And now I'm a public joke. They all poke fun at me. Every time I open my mouth I'm shouting, "Murder!" or "Rape!" And all I get for my GOD-warnings are insults and contempt. But if I say, "Forget it! No more GOD-Messages from me!" The words are fire in my belly, a burning in my bones." (Jeremiah 20:7-9 The Message)

As you may know - even at your age, life, school, sports, clubs - being a teenager, having friends, all these life responsibilities carry weight! Although they seem small to parents and older adults, these responsibilities sometimes tend to get hard to maintain and the easy thing is to quit.

In my life, God has allowed me to have and experience success in many areas including ministry. After 10 years serving in ministry, God transitioned me back to my hometown of Hazlehurst, Georgia to start a church called Empact Church of Hazlehurst. It has single-handedly been the hardest thing I've ever done in my life. Trying to *empact* (impact) a region that is drenched in tradition, overwhelmed with closed minds, and only remembers you as a child or a hardheaded teenager is hard. To make it plain, it has been hard. Although the ministry is still growing and the community *empact* (impact) is great, the envy, the closed minds, the competition, the hate, the unwillingness to understand, has oftentimes made me want to quit ministry altogether. Each time I think of quitting or giving up, this quote by Jeremiah sprints to the forefront of my mind, "But if I say, "Forget it! No more GOD-Messages from me!" The words are fire in my belly, a burning in my bones."

This is my motivation each time I think about quitting. Today, as you face the challenges of your teenage years, anytime quitting starts to creep in or when the better option seems to be to just walk away, let your fire and passion be the final push. Times are going to get hard, life will get heavy, some things will fail, friends will pull at you or pull away, breakups will happen, you will get mad with your parents, teachers, coaches or even your brothers and sisters. Let the passion in your bones burn in your belly! Don't quit! Quitting is not an option!

Day 24

FOLLOW THE LEADER

"Be strong and very courageous. Be careful to obey all the instructions Moses gave you. Do not deviate from them, turning either to the right or to the left. Then you will be successful in everything you do."
(Joshua 1:7 New Living Translation)

I've preached this verse several times, and it wasn't until I started writing this devotional that it hit me! When God makes a promise of success to Joshua and the children of God, God is actually telling them to follow instructions. This means that much of your success is based on how well you follow instructions. The main thing that caught my attention this time were the instructions God gave them to follow. These were the same instructions Moses, who was Joshua's mentor, gave them to follow. Why is this important? Simple. God isn't saying I'll give you success for following only my instructions. God is saying I promise you success if you follow the instructions of the leader. Following the instructions of the leader is a form of obedience. God chooses obedience over anything.

For decades, Moses served as the leader of God's people. God was instructing the new leader, Joshua, and the people, to follow the instructions laid out for them by the previous leader if they wanted to be successful. This teaches a valuable lesson. Success isn't based only on your work ethic! Success isn't only discovered in your connections! Success isn't only manifested through your prayers. What God is saying to us through this story is success is also based on your ability to follow the leader!

As a teenager today, this should be encouragement for you to get behind your leader and commit to following that leader. Success, if you want it, will be determined by your ability to follow a leader! Leadership will look different at different stages in your life, but if you ever master following the leader, success will always follow you! Even the best leaders are great followers.

Day 25

YOU'VE BEEN MARKED

"GOD told him, "No. Anyone who kills Cain will pay for it seven times over." GOD put a mark on Cain to protect him so that no one who met him would kill him." (Genesis 4:15 The Message)

I struggled with this theme or idea for this devotional. As I was searching through the Bible app in hopes that God will give me some motivation for writing, I saw Mike Todd's devotion titled "Marked". The first thought that came to mind was "Cray, you've been marked". This thought led me to Genesis chapter 4, and the story of Cain and Abel.

In Genesis chapter 4, Cain and Abel, the first sons of Adam and Eve, both brought offerings to God. They brought their offerings to God, but they brought them in two different ways with two different attitudes. This highlights what the Bible says about the attitude we should have when we give. The Bible says you should give what you have set in your hearts to give, and you should give it with a good attitude. In Genesis 4, Abel gives from the heart and with the right attitude. Cain gives reluctantly, and because of Cain's bad attitude, God rejects his offering causing Cain to become so jealous that he kills his brother Abel. When God exposes Cain's behavior and his sin, God punishes him, curses his work and his life journey. He would never be settled.

Cain, in a moment of vulnerability, confronts God about the severity of his punishment. He tells God his punishment is too harsh and that someone would eventually kill him. Then God assures Cain he would not be killed, and if someone did kill him, their punishment would be seven times worse. Then God placed a mark of protection on him. A mark that told all his enemies not to touch him. Cain lived to be 730 years old.

The point for us today, is just like Cain, when we have failures or shortcomings in a moment of weakness or vulnerability, God has marked us. Just like Cain, when God labels us as a child of God, God has marked us. Just like Cain, when we pray to God, God will hear us and mark us. Today should send a notice and reminder to you that you have been marked by God with the mark of protection, and that's why no weapon formed against you will be able to prosper simply because you have been marked.

Day 26

DON'T FORGET ABOUT GOD

"This I know: the favor that brings promotion and power doesn't come from anywhere on earth, for no one exalts a person but God, the true judge of all. He alone determines where favor rests. He anoints one for greatness and brings another down to his knees." (Psalm 75:6-7 The Passion Translation)

I remember in the early part of my ministry journey; I was studying the story of Jonah. You know the one that was swallowed by a whale. Yea, that Jonah. I was studying that story in preparation for Bible study on the campus of Troy University. One of the things that stood out to me was the fact that Jonah's punishment was based on his initial refusal to go where God told him to go. I couldn't understand it at the time, and I was so critical of Jonah's reason as to why he didn't want to go to where God told him to go. His reasoning was not good enough in my mind at the time. His reasoning was that he knew God's mercy, and he did not think the people of Nineveh deserved God's mercy. They knew who God was, what God could do, they even knew that it was God sparing them, but still they chose to do their own thing and they created a wicked city. Yet, God wanted to give them a chance to be forgiven and it would be through Jonah, but Jonah wasn't having it. He felt they deserved what they were earning and that was destruction. So, he refused to go!

When I think of Jonah's story, I now understand it. As a pastor, I understand exactly how he feels. I've watched people get blessed by God, find the love of their life after praying, get healed after praying, get financial breakthroughs after praying, pass tests after praying, excel at their sport after praying. At the moment they were blessed, they gradually faded away from God. They stop prioritizing church and Bible study attendance. They put their new shining stuff out front, and God on the back burner. I've seen this so often and like Jonah, I find myself not wanting to spiritually associate myself with them. Actually, it angers me, but I'm often reminded I'm not God. I'm just a vessel of God.

Today, I want to send a reminder to you. Please remember God. When you get blessed, healed, delivered. When the promotion comes, when the scholarship is secured, when you meet new friends, don't forget about God! Always remember to not forget about God! Put God first.

Day 27

GET UP AND DO SOMETHING

"When David noticed them whispering to each other, he realized that the child had died. So, he asked them, "Is the child dead?" "Yes, he is," they answered. David got up from the floor, took a bath, combed his hair, and changed his clothes. Then he went and worshiped in the house of the Lord. When he returned to the palace, he asked for food and ate it as soon as it was served." (2 Samuel 12:19-20 Good News Translation)

I preached a sermon one time titled "Get Your Mind Out the Gutter". I dealt with the story of David when he found himself stuck in a state of depression because of his behaviors. He had taken Bathsheba against her will. (You don't know who Bathsheba is? LOL. What's my saying? You should know by now. Google is your best friend.) Either way, David had taken this woman, Bathsheba, against the word of his leadership team and against the vows of her marriage and slept with her getting her pregnant. Like many of us when trouble strikes, he attempts to cover up his mess by having her husband killed and then marrying her. However, he could not escape the consequences of his behaviors. God sent a deadly illness on his child, and the child died. The entire time while the child was sick, David struggled. He didn't eat, he slept on the floor, he didn't take a bath, he isolated himself and he was suffering from situational depression. The story says after David heard that the child had died, he got up!

After our church service, our leadership team gathers to discuss the reflections about the sermon. I remember one of our team members highlighting that for him the most *empactful* (impactful) part of this story was that David got up! I want to push it a step further for you as a teenager reading this devotional. Not only did David get up from his situation, but he then took a bath, washed his face, combed his hair, changed his clothes, and went to church. In other words, David got up and did something about his situation.

My encouragement to you today is to not only get up from your situations but do something to change them. Whatever situation you've found yourself stuck in or simply experiencing, don't just stay there! Get up and do something!

Day 28
STOP TRYING TO IMPRESS PEOPLE

"My message and my preaching were not with wise and persuasive words, but with a demonstration of the Spirit's power, so that your faith might not rest on human wisdom, but on God's power." (1 Corinthians 2:4-5 New International Version)

After a full day of ministry and being up since early that morning, I fell asleep around 9:30 p.m. A couple hours later, I woke up around 11:30 p.m. I started cleaning up some, and then I decided to check out this sermon by Pastor Mike Todd called "Through the Rain, The Anchor Remains". In the message, Mike Todd mentions being impressive vs. *empactful* (impactful). He goes on to say that so many of us are more concerned with impressing people than we are with impacting people. I know you're probably thinking, "well as a teenager that doesn't matter much to me right now." But the fact that you are reading this book, especially since you have read it this far, would suggest it means something to you.

As I was listening, Pastor Mike Todd said something that got me together. He said, "what would the world look like if we stop caring about being impressive and doubled down on being *empactful*?" That got me and made me think about how I've shaped my words, actions and even thoughts, around the hope to impress family, friends, peers, and even people at our church. When I heard that it made me realize, "Cray, stop trying to impress people and focus on being *empactful*. Don't lose yourself or years of your life trying to impress people."

As I thought about this story, I thought about myself and one of my favorite scriptures from when I first started ministry. 1 Corinthians 2:4 states, "My words and my preaching aren't with persuasive words, but I preach and speak with power." This should be our example. We don't have to seek to impress people with our attire, our sermons, our singing, our intellect, our house, our car, our education. We should seek to *empact* (impact) people with the Spirit's power.

Today, realize and recognize that no matter how much you try to impress people, you'll never impress as many people as you can *empact* with the Spirit's power! Stop trying to be impressive and focus on being *empactful*.

Day 29

THEY SMILE IN YOUR FACE

"Some "friends" pretend to be friends, but a true friend sticks closer than a brother." (Mishlei (Proverbs) 18:24 Complete Jewish Bible)

I moved to California in November of 2020. My transition to California has been tough, hard, and challenging. And nearly one year later, it is still extremely tough. Some days are tougher than others. One particular day was a really tough day. I called my mentor searching for insight and comfort, but after our conversation it just really darkened the day even more. When I woke up the next morning, I started reading my Bible and found myself at Proverbs 18:24. I stumbled upon the Complete Jewish Bible translation. Scripture states, "Some "friends" pretend to be friends, but a true friend sticks closer than a brother."

Some "friends" pretend to be friends - whew! That's the part that hit me. It made me think about a song by this old group called The O'Jays. This song was before my time, so it was certainly before your time. But Google is your best friend. Google them. The song is called "Back Stabbers". The lyrics say:

> *"They smilin' in your face*
> *All the time, they want to take your place*
> *The back stabbers"*

And in a moment of laughter and pettiness, I felt like I was privately clowning them in my head - those who smile in my face and pretend to be my friends. Then, God switched it up on me. God took me through the last several months of my life. God showed me - with memories - all the times I've covered up hurt, pain, frustration, aggravation (and so much more) with a smile on my face. Instantly, the song lyrics became about me. "They smilin' in your face". "They" were me - wearing a smile like a Band-Aid trying to cover my pain.

Why is this relevant to you, you ask? Because you as a teenager may be wearing a mask. No pun intended. Parents can't tell, teachers can't tell, friends can't. Everyone can see your smile, not knowing it's just a mask to cover your pains. Smiling through hurts, smiling through disappointments, smiling through frustrations, smiling through failed opportunities. You are smiling in their face while silently falling apart!

From a masked smiler to another, I encourage you today through the second part of Proverbs 18:24, "But a true friend sticks closer than a brother." That friend is Jesus! When trouble comes and you are tired of wearing the fake smile, you can give your issues to Jesus.

Day 30

LEAVE IT WITH THE LORD

"So, here's what I've learned through it all: Leave all your cares and anxieties at the feet of the Lord, and measureless grace will strengthen you." (Psalm 55:22 The Passion Translation)

I'm 37 years old. My teenage years passed me by a while ago, but I've learned the longer we live, the more certain we are to have trouble in our lives. You will learn this too. All types of life troubles, car trouble, relationship trouble, school troubles, friendship trouble, trouble at home, trouble at your church. If there is one absolute in this life - outside of being born and facing death - is that we will have troubles. The unfortunate part of having troubles is that there is no prediction of when trouble is going to happen, and there is no formula to getting rid of trouble.

We grew up singing an old church song that says, "trouble don't last always." I never understood the true purpose of the song's lyrics because the song says, "I'm so glad, that trouble don't last always". The thing that bothers me the most is that although those lyrics are very encouraging, there is no solution mentioned. I've always wondered: are we supposed to just wait and let our troubles run their course, or is there a strategy to getting rid of our troubles?

Well, fortunate enough for us, Psalm 55:22 has given us the formulas for handling our troubles. It states for us to leave our troubles at the feet of the Lord. Now this gives us an even greater reason for why we should attend church. There is an altar at your church. (That's usually the place upfront in the church.) When we go there and pray, leave your troubles there. When you leave church, you should be leaving your troubles. When you finish praying, you should be leaving your troubles. When you leave worship, after praising God, you should be leaving your troubles. When you leave Bible study, you should be leaving your troubles with the Lord.

Today, leave your stress, your anxieties, your pain, your brokenness. Leave your hurt, leave your feelings, leave it all at the feet of Jesus. When we leave all our troubles and anxieties at the feet of the Lord, the Lord's grace that never runs out will strengthen us.

www.ingramcontent.com/pod-product-compliance
Lightning Source LLC
Chambersburg PA
CBHW050448010526
44118CB00013B/1733